Fear
Overcome Fear

Strategies For Eliminating Fear From Your Life

By Ace McCloud
Copyright © 2014

Disclaimer

The information provided in this book is designed to provide helpful information on the subjects discussed. This book is not meant to be used, nor should it be used, to diagnose or treat any medical condition. For diagnosis or treatment of any medical problem, consult your own physician. The publisher and author are not responsible for any specific health or allergy needs that may require medical supervision and are not liable for any damages or negative consequences from any treatment, action, application or preparation, to any person reading or following the information in this book. Any references included are provided for informational purposes only. Readers should be aware that any websites or links listed in this book may change.

Table of Contents

Introduction 6

Chapter 1: Breathing Techniques and Other Physical Methods to Prevent and Conquer Fear 9

Chapter 2: Mental Preparations to Combat Fear 13

Chapter 3: Fighting Fear With Natural Supplements, Drugs and A Proper Diet 18

Chapter 4: Create an Action Plan to Prevent or Control Fear 23

Conclusion 27

My Other Books and Audio Books 28

Be sure to check out my website for all my Books and Audio books.

www.AcesEbooks.com

Introduction

I want to thank you and congratulate you for buying this book: "Over Come Fear- Strategies for Eliminating Fear from Your Life."

This book contains proven steps and strategies on how to overcome fear and live a more enjoyable and fulfilling life.

Fear is a part of our being when we are born and stays with us until death. This self-preservation reaction keeps us safe, but it can also impede us from our success. Everyone has fears. It is how you deal with them that matters.

Some people ignore their fears and blast their way through life. They experience new things; they are considered to be confident and are seen as being courageous. Wouldn't it be great if your hands didn't sweat or your voice didn't quiver when you ask your boss for a raise? Wouldn't it be wonderful to stand on a high, rocky cliff and dive down into the deep ocean? Your fears might be holding you back from truly enjoying your life.

This book will help you to overcome your fears and manage the symptoms of high heart rate, high blood pressure and the lack of control that can happen when fear strikes. It will help you to understand what fear is and how to calm its symptoms. We will also explore how fear affects your life and your success. This book will try to help you to be more self-confident so that you have the best chance for a successful and fear free life.

Let's face it. Most of our fears are irrational. Remember those monsters that hid in the closet when you were a kid? They were clearly irrational fears. Being afraid of flying or being in a confined area are real fears for some people. Although they are more realistic than monsters in the closet, they are still irrational. Sure, airplanes do crash, but what is the likelihood yours will? Chances are very small that this will happen to you, and worrying about it is a waste of your brain power. Some people are very afraid of elevators. But how many people are actually injured in an elevator? You have a better chance of walking across the street and being hit by a truck than being injured in an elevator accident.

Fear is an insidious problem. Many times, you may not even know that you have a fear issue until something happens and you find yourself dealing with its chilly effects. It is important to understand fear and how to face it. See this YouTube video: "5 Tricks for Overcoming Fear" by watchwellcast to get an idea on what fear is and some methods for conquering it.

Eleanor Roosevelt gave some great advice on fear. She said, "You gain strength, courage, and confidence by every experience in which you really stop to look fear in the face. You are able to say to yourself, 'I have lived through this horror. I can take the next thing that comes along.' You must do the thing you think you cannot do." These are wise words from a wise woman. She tells us that when we face our fears, we receive three positive qualities in return. They are strength, courage and confidence. All are essential to make you a success in life and help you overcome fear.

Fear has a tendency to keep you stuck where you are and does not allow you to progress any further in your development until the fear is overcome. Someone who is afraid of lightning and thunder will continue to be afraid of it if they don't do something about it. They might hide in a closet or under their bed until the storm is over. They might miss an event like a family reunion or an outing with friends merely because there is supposed to be bad weather. This person is stuck and can easily miss out on enjoyable events as long as they give in to the fear. William Barth discusses his own experience with fear and how he conquered it in this YouTube video posted by TheWarriorSage, Self-Awareness 101 Episode 37 - What Is Fear?.

When considering fear, the brain is first concerned with how it can fight fear or how it can avoid and run from it. This is called "the fight or flight reaction". This reaction was a good thing in the ancient past because the early world did not have the protections we have today. There was no order, no police and no supermarkets. It was the early human being's job to find enough food to sustain life and not become dinner for another predator. The fight or flight reaction was necessary in ancient days to keep humans alive.

There is a small, almond shaped pod in the middle of the human brain called the amygdala and it is the part of the brain that processes our first reaction to fear. When fear strikes, the amygdala speeds up the heart and makes muscles tense up in anticipation of fight or flight. This is the most primitive part of the brain and it is also present in animal brains. Fortunately, humans have two other brain areas that animals don't and these areas allow for calming the response in order to manage it. The amygdala is often called "The lizard's brain" because the lizard only has the ability of discerning fight or flight when confronted with fear. The trick to overcoming fear is to move out of the lizard's brain and into the other sections of the brain that help us to process fear and see it for what it really is.

That might sound easy, but for some people, the task is very difficult. They might be faced with fear and freeze. They might run or cry or do things they would not normally do. A teenager might have taken all the driver education classes they need and even been in a driving simulator, but when they actually take the wheel, they can't bring themselves to put their foot down on the accelerator because fear is stopping them. It is also preventing them to learn how to drive. It is important for the teenager to get past this fear and learn to drive so they can go on to make a successful life for themselves.

The amygdala is an important part of both human and animal brain. It keeps us alive in some cases and warns us to danger. Unfortunately for us, it is very adept at finding danger even in the most benign situations. It is important for humans to process fear past the amygdala and recognize that the fear is irrational and what is happening to them at the moment is not going to hurt or kill them. I look forward to sharing with you an abundance of knowledge that will certainly help you in overcoming fears that are present in your own life.

Chapter 1: Breathing Techniques and Other Physical Methods to Prevent and Conquer Fear

Breathing and other physical movements and exercises can have a positive effect on our whole being. They also go a long way to helping us overcome our fears. Here are some of the most popular methods.

Yoga

Yoga is the perfect exercise to do in order to help stop panic and fear. Yoga is a combination of breathing and movement. It is an ancient practice that melds together the body, mind and spirit. Breathing is very important in Yoga because it prepares the brain to be calm. The different stretches and poses of yoga center the body and make it stronger and more balanced. Another part of Yoga is meditation. Meditation is used to link the spirit to the mind and the body. Many practitioners run thorough a litany of mantras and positive affirmations while meditating, posing and breathing and this can reinforce confidence and overcome fear. When you do your exercises repeat your positive affirmation mantras to banish fear. For example, if you are afraid of crowded areas a good affirmation to repeat could be: "I enjoy being around others and people like me." The repetition of the mantra wiggles into the subconscious mind in a positive manner and you might find yourself gravitating towards crowded areas with no problems at all.

Breathing

Mothers-to-be are taught breathing exercises in order to deal with the pain of child birth. There is a good reason for that. It is a great way to stay calm and relax as much as possible when in labor so that everything goes smoothly. Deep breathing slows the heart rate, relaxes muscles and demands concentration. Yoga breathing also deals with deep breathing and does similar things.

The following exercises are easy for anyone to accomplish because you can lie on the floor or on a bed, or sit in a chair while doing them.

Basic Breathing

1. Lie flat on your back, raise your knees and put your feet flat on the floor or on the bed.
2. Place one hand, palm down, on the abdomen right under the ribs and breathe as you normally would for one minute.
3. Relax and breathe deeply, pausing between each breath. Notice if your hand rises and falls with each intake of breath. If your shoulders are going

up and down instead, you are not using the diaphragm, and not breathing to your full potential. The diaphragm is a circle of muscle that is right under the ribs and goes around from front to back. When you breathe in through your nose, the diaphragm should move out and raise your hand. When you exhale out through the mouth, the hand and diaphragm should go in.

4. Try breathing using the diaphragm. It should be easier lying down than sitting up because when reclining there is pressure against the back and allows the diaphragm to work better. Your hand goes up and the diaphragm goes out when you inhale and the hand goes down and diaphragm goes in when exhaling.

5. Once you get the idea of breathing correctly, you can continue. You should already feel a bit relaxed. Perform six breaths and hold your breath between the inhale and the exhale. Breathe in and out slowly.

Avoid breathing too quickly or over doing it because you can cause hyperventilation, which makes it feel like you are suffocating or like you are very light headed.

Do this exercise at least once a day and gradually increase from six breaths to 12 breaths over time.

Another breathing exercise draws air across the tongue and causes a cool sensation that calms the nervous system. Do it while sitting in a chair or by sitting cross legged on the floor.

Cool Breath Breathing

1. Stick the tongue out of the mouth and curl the sides of it up. Your tongue should look like a roll or straw.

2. Lift the chin up pointing to the ceiling.

3. Breathe in using the diagram and draw air through the tongue.

4. Hold the breath for a few seconds, uncurl the tongue and move it back into the mouth.

5. Exhale through the nostrils and move the chin down.

Do this exercise six times and gradually increase to twelve times over time. The more practice you get in, the more ingrained this exercise will imprint on your brain. After it has become a habit, it will be an automatic response to fear once you get used to it.

The YouTube video "Healing Through Yoga: Releasing Fear and Anxiety" by Jasmine Kaloudes, shows how the stomach and abdomen look when you breathe from the diaphragm. It shows how the diaphragm moves out and in when you breathe correctly.

These breathing exercises take concentration and that helps in relieving fear. It gives your brain something else to think about other than the fear.

Tensing Exercise

Another exercise where concentration is involved is the tense exercise. When fear strikes your muscles tend to involuntarily tense. In the tense exercise, you tense your muscles to get them tied into knots as if you were in a fear situation. Then you learn to gradually relax those muscles, which also takes some concentration and distracts the brain from fear itself.

1. Lie down flat on the floor or on the bed.
2. Breathe in deeply, using the diaphragm and hold your breath.
3. Purposely tense the muscles in your head, neck and shoulders and count to ten.
4. Let the breath out slowly and force the muscles in the neck and shoulders to relax gradually starting at the neck and going to the upper arms.
5. Do the same with the arms and hands. Then relax from the upper arm down to the tips of the fingers.
6. Proceed with the tensing exercise to the trunk of the body starting at the chest and back down, working toward the hips. Pay special attention to the stomach.
7. Continue from the hips and buttocks down to your toes.

Do the breathing and tensing exercises once a day and when fear takes hold, begin to do them immediately. The breathing and tensing should stop the fear induced raised heart rate and muscle tensing and allow you to move the fear from the fight or flight lizard brain to the upper parts of the brain where it can be recognized as irrational.

Learn how to stop anxiety and fear in all kinds of situations, from human encounters to being stuck in an elevator. The techniques in the YouTube video, How to Calm Down in 10 Seconds (Fast Relaxation Trick to Stop Anxiety and Stress) by ALifeLessAnxious includes a great example of the breathing and tensing exercises.

If you can't seem to automatically start the breathing exercises, keep a regular, large sized blow up balloon in your pocket. When panic starts, take it out and blow it up. This will automatically stop swift breathing and can help alleviate the panic symptoms.

Utilize breathing and tensing techniques whenever fear takes hold. An example would be for those afraid of confined areas. Maybe you need to have an MRI.

Even open MRI machines can send a person screaming into the night. You lie between two hard surfaces and the top one is almost on top of you. You can't sit up, you can't turn and you can't escape. My brother does not like confined spaces and when encountering his first MRI, he just couldn't do it. He cried, hyperventilated and both the technician and he gave up. It didn't matter that it was safe, the fear was completely irrational. He was more prepared the second time around after learning the breathing and tensing techniques. He asked for a fan to blow air onto his face so it didn't feel like he was suffocating. After being inserted into the open MRI, he closed his eyes and asked them to wait a moment while he did the breathing and tensing exercises. After a few minutes he was calm and was able to get the procedure done.

Physical Exercise

Simply doing something physical like pushups, sit ups, or jumping jacks can also stop fear from setting in. While you are doing them, count to occupy the brain. Another good idea is to burn energy constructively by exercising or cleaning the house.

The University of Georgia performed a study that analyzed 40 clinical trials associated with medical and mental conditions. The study found that patients who participated in regular exercise sessions reduced the anxiety they had by about 20 percent. These patients had fewer symptoms of worry and fear than those that did not exercise. They also found that those that exercised regularly 30 minutes or more per day were much more adept at reducing fear and anxiety by themselves. Physical exercise can help many people with overcoming fear.

Exercise releases endorphins, which are hormones that make you feel good. Regular exercises releases these hormones regularly and results in making you feel you can take on the world, and your fear. If you would like to know more about this, be sure to check out my bestselling book: [Ultimate Health Secrets](#).

Chapter 2: Mental Preparations to Combat Fear

Fear is merely a mental perception of an external stimulus that can be extremely uncomfortable. Fear of fire can keep you safe. The realization that the house is on fire causes fear in most people and they immediately jump into action and get out to safety. However, fear of lighting matches is in a way related to the fear of fire but is most irrational as lighting a match cannot hurt you much. You might get a little burn, but the flame from the match is very easy to put out. The fear of lighting a match is purely a mental issue as there is no real serious danger. These types of fears are best dealt with head on as they serve no useful purpose in your life.

Preparing to deal with fear is something everyone should do whether you have irrational fear or not. It helps you to see your fears for what they really are and by doing so allows you to be much faster in ascertaining if a situation is life threatening or not. This preparation includes making lists, questioning, observing and changing.

Lists and Other Written Exercises

Sit down and make a list of your interests, your strengths, values and your dreams. Use this to write a positive biography about yourself. This can be very important in the future, so take five minutes to do this now! Now make a list of those things that can make fear arise in yourself. Now look at both lists and you can see that your fears do not match your positive biography. You may have give yourself the qualities of being level-headed, confident and honest. Your fears may include a fear of flying or fear of elevators. You can see that these do not match. Your fears look pretty silly for a level-headed, confident person and it is time to get honest about them.

Developing a curiosity about your fear may help in banishing or reducing it. Curious people are enthusiastic and want to learn something new. Open your fears to your natural curiosity and you might find them more of a learning experience than a horror. Curiosity distracts the mind from the actual fear. It helps you to learn about it and once you inspect the situation, the fear may disappear. Write down some questions about your fear and then try to answer them as if you were talking to someone else about those fears.

Questions might include:
1. Why am I afraid to fly?
2. What happened that made me afraid to fly?
3. What does it feel like when I know I have to get on an airplane?
4. How can I make myself more comfortable while inside an airplane?

Answer those questions as best you can and if the answer to #4 is to know how the mechanics of a plane works, then you can spend some time researching that and the safety records or various different types of planes.

In the YouTube video, Secret to Overcoming Fear by Dr. Michael J. Duckett, the importance of written word to combat fear is discussed. The Doctor gives some good suggestions on how to get "un-stuck" when writing down feelings and lists.

Make a Fear Board

You can make a fear board by writing different fears on cards or sticky notes and putting them on a bulletin board as if you were in a CSI crime lab. Add other cards on techniques to banish these fears and try them out one by one. This gives you a visual aid to help you understand what you need to do to stop fears from affecting your life.

Visualization Exercises

Visualization is a form of meditation that can make a real difference in most people. Some of the most prominent people in society today use visualization as a tool for success and that makes it a great tool to conquer fear.

Conquering Fear

1. Lie down or sit comfortably.
2. Do some deep breathing and count each breath. This will stop that internal dialog we all have inside our heads.
3. Imagine yourself in a fear situation. If you are afraid of water, imagine yourself floating in a cool blue pool without any trouble. You will not fall below the water and the water will not fill your lungs. You are able to swim and even if someone plays a trick on you and pushes you under, you have the ability to rise above the water and start floating again.

Go to Your Calm Place

Most people have a favorite place where they feel most comfortable and confident. It might be the beach, it might be the backyard of your childhood home where you spent most of your summer in your tree house, it could be the garden where you grow flowers and vegetables or a fantasy castle where you rule a mighty kingdom. Visualize this place and your heart rate will come down almost immediately. Practice going to your calm place so that when fear strikes you can get there without having to force yourself to think about it. The immediate symptoms of fear should go away quickly and you can then ascertain if the fear was life threatening or irrational.

Change the Way You Think

Changing the perception of your fear is another mental exercise that may help you to see how silly the fear really is and give you the strength to overcome it. Everyone has an internal dialog going on in their minds. When you become fearful, stop the negative dialog and change it to a positive one. When that airplane takes off change the internal dialog from "I'm going to crash and die" to "I'm going on a great adventure and see things I've never seen before".

Give Thanks

Gratitude is a powerful tool to battle fear. No matter what kind of mood you may be in, once you start to consider all the things you are grateful for, your mood changes. After going through the list you should no longer be scared or angry and the world will look a lot brighter. Sit or lie in a comfortable position, close your eyes and think of everything positive you have in your life. You can also write them down if you prefer. You might be grateful for having a nice home or car. You might be thankful for your family and pets or that you have more than a few bucks in your bank account. You can be thankful for easy access to water, a powerful military to protect you, abundant food, doctors to help take care of you, television that brings you your favorite programs, the computer which gives you powers that kings of old could only dream of. The list is nearly endless of all the things you can be grateful for. Once you start thinking of everything you have, your fears sort of melt away.

Confront Fear/Exposure Therapy

The amygdala or lizard brain learns by what you feel and by example. If you were once bit by a dog, the amygdala learns to be afraid of dogs and won't stop until you prove it wrong or do something to stop it. Positive exposure to dogs will help it to learn that you do not have to be afraid and your fear will eventually stop. No longer will seeing a dog send a message to increase your heart rate and initiate the fight or flight response. If you run away every time you see a dog, you will continue to be afraid of them and you may even encourage a few to chase you. Exposure therapy helps train the amygdala part of the brain to fear no longer. In exposure therapy, you confront your fears on a gradual basis where the object of fear cannot harm you. Pretty soon the amygdala ignores the fear and it no longer affects you.

Teaching a child not to be afraid of the water takes a great deal of patience, but soon they will be swimming with all the other kids instead of screaming and crying on the shore. The first day of the confrontation the child tends to sit around the edge of the pool with a parent and never get in. They can see the other kids having fun but they do not have the courage to get in themselves. The next day, the child is persuaded to sit on the edge and wiggle their toes in the water. No one should splash the child or threaten to push him or her in. You might even convince the child to let you pour water from the pool down their back to help cool them off. The next trip to the pool, the child gets in the shallow end with the parent and goes to the knees. The adult is trusted and they gradually guide the child deeper but to where the feet still stay on the bottom of the pool. Nothing bad has happened so far, so the child trusts nothing will. Next the child is convinced to put their face in the water, and then put the head in. When everything goes smoothly the child will be swimming and playing with the other kids in no time.

In any situation, once trust is earned and you know nothing bad is going to happen, you can progress to the next step. You wouldn't just throw a kid in the pool to confront fear, so you shouldn't put on a fire suit and wade through a fire ball to confront your fear of fire. Take it slow and have patience when confronting fear and you will go a long way in combating and eliminating your fears.

Another technique is to confront your fear by screaming at it. Sometimes getting really angry at fear will knock it right out of your consciousness. When panic hits, call the fear a name and tell it exactly what you think of it. It is probably best to do this when you are alone as others might think it to be strange. Visualize your fear as a big ball of darkness, mentally grab it, tell it to leave you alone and throw it over a mental cliff or into the sun. This method works well for confrontational people that can think in the abstract.

Hypnosis

Hypnosis can be a great way to banish fears. Hypnosis gives your mind suggestions that fools the lizard brain and makes fear by pass it completely. You can make an appointment with a professional or my favorite method is to listen to a hypnosis download on a regular basis. A great source for these types of audio recordings is HypnosisDownloads. Some good choices are: overcome fear and anxiety, overcome fear of failure, overcome fear of death, and much more.

Emotional Freedom Technique or Tapping

Emotional Freedom Technique or EFT is similar to acupuncture except you use your fingers instead of needles. This technique is said to be helpful when combating fear. You use your fingers to tap certain pressure points instead of inserting needles. The tapping takes the energy from your fingers and infuses it into those pressure points to banish fear. There are 12 pressure points used in this tapping technique and this method works for more issues than just fear, both mental and physical. EFT handbooks are easily downloaded from the Internet and the method works well for many. See this YouTube video by Mercola for an Emotional Freedom Technique (EFT) Demonstration.

Counseling

Some people have fears that are so ingrained; they can't get rid of them. In this case, it is best to consult a counselor. Those that are especially fearful of many things and cannot function in society need the extra help a counselor can provide. They should not be expected to try to overcome fears by themselves.

Negativity effects of Procrastination

Procrastination is a supreme road block where fear is involved. What better way for that lizard brain to stay just the way it is? Just sitting around and worrying about fear isn't going to get anything done. Get up and start doing something to alleviate your fears. Even if it is one simple thing done each day, over time this can really add up!

Many give fear way too much attention and control over their lives. Examining and observing our fears can lessen the effect of fear on us and confronting fear can often make them look silly enough to ignore them or have them just disappear.

Chapter 3: Fighting Fear With Natural Supplements, Drugs and A Proper Diet

Anxiety and panic are both a result of fear and both are treatable with natural supplements, vitamins, drugs and diet. It's a good idea to try a natural supplement first, but be aware that they also can have some negative side effects. If you take other prescription drugs, it is a good idea to consult a medical professional to make sure nothing will counteract what you are already taking or that the supplement won't affect a physical condition you currently have.

There is no pill that works right away to dispel fear. Most supplements and drugs have to course through the body for a few weeks and build up before they start to work. This takes some patience and there is a chance that what works for one person, will not work for another.

Herbal Supplements

St. John's Wort is probably the most well-known herb that combats anxiety and depression. The active ingredient in the herb is hypericin, which can lift spirits. St. John's Wort works a bit quicker than other remedies at a few weeks rather than a few months. The supplement is easily found in capsule form in pharmacies or health food stores. St. John's Wort tends to reduce effectiveness of birth control and increases the chance of sun sensitivity causing the likelihood of sunburn.

Kava is a substance that reduces anxiety, but it takes over eight weeks to start working. It has also been associated with liver and nerve damage when large amounts are ingested. Kava has sedative effects and the roots are ground and put into capsules. Avoid Kava if you are pregnant or breast feeding.

Valerian Root promotes sleep and relaxes the body and mind. It is effective against anxiety and insomnia. The herb smells pretty bad, so if you make tea, mix it with mint or another strong scented and flavored herb. It is best to use the capsule instead of the tea if you can't stand the smell. Taking too much Valerian can cause extreme drowsiness in some people.

An herb similar to Kava, but less strong is **Passion Flower**. Get this in capsule form to calm nerves. Passion flower contains beta-carboline hormala alkaloids, which have antidepressant properties. This herb will not help much with someone who has severe fear problems.

Catnip puts some cats into a temporary euphoria and is easy to grow if you can keep the cats away from it. Make tea from the leaves or get capsules. The oils in catnip dispel anxiety and may help keep fear on lower levels.

Chamomile tea is a calming drink and a natural sedative. The little yellow-centered, daisy-like flower is very effective in calming the body. Those with hay fever may get a rash when ingesting chamomile and they also might get a stuffy nose or burning eyes. Try just a little at first to see if it will bother you and if not, you can have as much of this pleasant tasting tea as you like. You might want to wait until bedtime or you may be yawning at work.

Skullcap is an herbal supplement used for those with restless leg syndrome to calm the nerves in the legs. It relaxes muscles and has sedative affects. It can also help those with anxiety and panic attacks. Avoid skullcap if you are pregnant.

The scent of lavender calms emotions, relaxes muscles and calms the mind. Keep oil of lavender ready to sniff or apply on the forehead when anxiety and fear strikes. A great lavender oil is: Now Foods Lavender and my favorite way to dispense it is with this essential oil diffuser.

Vitamins and Other Supplements

Vitamin B is thought to alleviate the propensity of panic attacks and it affects nerve function and mood. Vitamin B deficiency is common in many people, so a supplement can help raise the levels. Vitamin B1 controls blood sugar while B3 creates serotonin, which aids in sleep. Even blood sugar goes a long way to control mood and helps to combat anxiety while Serotonin brings the person tranquility. Vitamin B5 helps adrenal function and B12 is thought to combat depression. Try a B-complex supplement for best results. A good supplement to try is Nature Made Super B Complex.

Vitamin D is another vitamin found deficient in many people, especially in cities. We don't spend as much time outside as our ancestors did, so we may need a supplement. Vitamin D is essential in helping to release anxiety. The only way to find a deficiency is by taking a blood test as there are usually no symptoms. Your physician can prescribe high doses of Vitamin D and don't be surprised if you take 50,000 IU per week. A good over the counter choice is Now Foods Vitamin D.

Magnesium has the ability to help with high heart rate and rapid breathing created by fear. It also helps to keep blood pressure within the normal range and keep the heart rhythm steady. It is very useful for counteracting the effects of stress. Magnesium is thought to improve brain patterns and that in turn helps a person think more logically about fear and can help them to not dwell on past fear episodes. Take supplements or take a bath with ¼ cup of Epsom Salts dissolved in warm water that will absorb through the skin and give you the benefits. A good magnesium supplement is: Natural Calm Vitality.

GABA is an acronym for gamma-aminobutyric acid. This acid calms the nervous system, especially when stressed. When fears consume life, it impedes the production of GABA. Deficiencies cause anxiety, manic episodes and a propensity to alcoholism. You may also have headaches and heart palpitations. Nuts, broccoli, spinach, bananas, citrus and green tea aid in the production of GABA, but you can also take 500 to 1000 mg per day of the supplement.

L-Theanine (Green Tea)
Green tea has many benefits including the ability to keep the heart rate and blood pressure controlled in some people. Green tea is a healthy addition to any diet. You can take it in capsule form or in tea form. The theanine in green tea also raises GABA levels and has the added advantage of protecting you from environmental neurotoxins.

Omega-3, or fish oil, is a supplement that strengthens the heart and can help dispel depression. Omega-3 oil helps make for a healthy body and mind. Omega-3 oil comes from fatty fish, but if you don't like fish, you can take organic fish oil supplements. If you have any inflammations including pain in joints or an open sore, Omega-3 will help these too. A great Omega-3 supplement is: [Kirkland Natural Fish Oil](#).

Drugs
Some people need a little more help when it comes to fears and anxiety and may have to take pharmaceutical drugs to take care of them. Most drugs have hefty side effects, so only take them under a physician's watch.

Anti-anxiety drugs have been found to provide temporary relief for fear and anxiety, but they are not a cure. Many anti-anxiety drugs have unpleasant side effects and can become addictive. They can also take a good amount of time to take effect, as my little sister discovered when we visited Cancun Mexico on a family vacation. She is afraid of flying and so took her prescription anti-anxiety pill about fifteen minutes before takeoff. When the plane was about to take off, she still did not feel the effects of her medication, so she took another pill. Everything went smoothly, but it wasn't until about an thirty minutes into the flight before the medication took effect, at which point she could barely talk and walk. It is always a good idea to be extremely careful when taking prescription medications and I personally go to great lengths to avoid them whenever possible.

Common Prescription Medications

Tranquilizers or benzodiazepines slow down the central nervous system and results in relaxation. The names of some of these drugs include Xanax (alprazolam), Klonopin (clonazepam), Valium (diazepam) and Ativan (lorazepam). These drugs work quickly; in less than one hour after taking them. They slow brain activity and most people become sleepy or foggy and may slur their speech or be uncoordinated after taking them. These drugs are taken as needed and their properties are released from the system slowly and can easily build up in the body. They also tend to be very addictive and have been the downfall of many people.

Antidepressants like Prozac, Zoloft, Paxil, Lexipro and Celexa regulate the serotonin in the brain, which improves mood and the ability to handle fear. Antidepressants also cause nausea, nervousness, dizziness and extreme fatigue. You have to take these drugs on a regular schedule and withdrawal is likely when stopping.

Beta-Blockers are normally used for heart issues or blood pressure, but they also block effects of the stress hormone norepinephrine. This is the hormone that regulates the fight or flight response of the lizard brain.

Diet

Believe it or not, diet can positively reflect on your power to overcome fear. Blood sugar swings cause anxiety and create issues with panic and fear. Sugar and caffeine directly affect the flight or fight reaction. To decrease the chance of fear or panic, increase complex carbohydrates in your diet. Eat smaller meals more frequently to keep blood sugar level steady. You should also drink plenty of water to keep the body hydrated and limit caffeine, sugar and alcohol.

If you are a vegetarian, you might want to start eating a little meat or take supplements. Liver, beef and turkey give the body magnesium while beef, chicken and fish like halibut or salmon infuse the body with B vitamins. These fish also help supply Omega-3 oil.

Vegetables and fruits also give you the necessary minerals and vitamins needed to fight fear. Potatoes and bananas are rich in Vitamin B and spinach, kale, chard, watermelon, figs and green beans are filled with Vitamin D.

Dairy products tend to reduce anxiety and stress because of the calcium they contain. Yogurt is a great choice of food because it also helps you to digest your food easier.

Complex Carbohydrates take longer than other foods to digest and they turn into sugar that gives the body energy. Try whole grains, whole wheat pasta, oats and bran.

Sugar is generally a no-no when combating fear. It can make you jumpy with excess energy. A good substitute is dark chocolate which has tryptophan in it, which changes to serotonin. Peanut butter is also helpful in creating tryptophan.

Herbs like ginger, peppermint and chamomile make a great tea, but they also help with anxiety. They can help settle a tense stomach and make you feel less stressed.

The goal is to eat a healthy diet to prevent fear from overcoming your life. For more advanced information on being as healthy as you possibly can be, check out my **bestselling book:** Ultimate Health Secrets.

Chapter 4: Create an Action Plan to Prevent or Control Fear

Having a plan to combat fear is advantageous, so that when fear does rear its ugly head, you know exactly what you should be doing to combat it. You should be practicing your favorite fear fighting techniques every day, so that when the time comes, the process you use to beat fear back is so ingrained in your mind that it automatically kicks in.

An action plan to conquer fear is good to have when it comes to your future, your education, your job and in life as you will most likely be combating fear till the game of life is over. An action plan causes your vision or dream to seem a little more realistic and explains what you must do to move toward a goal. Once you know what to do and have a plan set in place, fear will naturally subside.

An action plan sets you up for success rather than allowing you to wallow in procrastination or a failure mindset. When you have an action plan, you are less likely to forget something and when you do have one, all the details of your vision are right there before you. You need to write your action plan once you decide once and for all that you want to conquer your fears and have tried several methods that have worked successfully to get rid of them.

Develop your action plan on paper and put it on your refrigerator or bulletin board, tape it to your closet door in the bedroom or put it on the wall in the bathroom. It needs to be somewhere that is out in the open and that you can see every day. Look at it every chance you get to reinforce the steps necessary so that they become familiar and ingrained in your subconscious. Memorize your action plan so that you can retrieve it any time that you need it. Once the plan is memorized, visualization is an incredible tool to utilize. Just picture yourself in the 3rd person, as if from a distance away, perfectly executing your action plan to conquer any fear that may be trying to take hold. The more you do this, the more of a pro you will become at fighting fear.

The steps in your action plan need to be very specific and detailed. Avoid writing down just the title of the method. Instead, write the whole procedure and specifics of the method. Write down the steps and concentrate on the goal. You might even give yourself a time when this goal needs to be completed, but be realistic. If you make the time frame too small you could become discouraged because you aren't reaching it as fast as you thought you would. A good technique to use when making goals is to add the words: "I will easily..." to the beginning of each goal.

An example of a good working action plan is as follows:

Create a goal - Maybe it is a long-term goal like "I will easily get on an airplane in six months and take a flight" or it might be "I will easily be able to stop my fear of confined places if I am forced to be in one".

Step 1 - Start out with simple breathing exercises that work best for you.

Step 2 - Add the tensing method to your plan if you are in a convenient place to utilize it.

Step 3 - If going to your calm place helps to calm your fears, then go ahead and put this in the plan. Write a vivid description of your calm place so that you can bring it up even if you start to panic. When you write, the information goes right into the storage area of the brain and is easy to access when you need it.

If yelling at your fears and calling them names works for you, then put this in the plan and yell your head off. Write a description of what you are going to do. Imagine the fear looking like a big black ball. Confront the ball and call it some choice names. Tell it to go away and never come back. Tell it how it is ruining your life and mentally catch the ball of fear and throw it as hard as you can over a cliff or into the sun.

Step 4 - Try to reason with your fear. Write questions you would ask to yourself like: Why are you panicking? Is there really a reason to panic? Is there a simple solution? Look for that simple solution by comparing, doing what is second nature or pulling from your past.

Step 5 - Take control. Throw out all negative thoughts and be proactive. Get yourself out of the situation or accept it and do the best you can. Then move on. Realize you do have control and use it.

Step 6 – Actively eat healthy, take good supplements, visualize regularly, use a hypnosis download daily, read the vision board daily, exercise, and watch and use some of the great "Tapping" videos on YouTube.

Step 7 - This is the best step of the whole plan. Celebrate once the fear subsides. Treat yourself because you deserve it. Celebrating enhances courage and confidence. When the situation arises and fear starts to take hold, you can concentrate on the celebration instead of the fear. Think about how you will celebrate. Maybe you will treat yourself to ice cream or a steak dinner. You might want to celebrate by going out with friends or relatives or you might enjoy taking the time to curl up with a good book or movie. Write whatever your celebration plan is down so your consciousness feels that it is more real than just words on paper.

Make at least one step in the action plan measurable so you can see progress. It might be, "I will be able to calm myself in 1 minute" or "I will be able to think rationally and disregard fear in 2 minutes". Most action plans have time lines and you can add those to yours. Perhaps you want to be successful in breathing and tensing by a certain date. The only problem with this is that the fear situation might not crop up during that time limit. You are not working with something that happens every day. You can, however, put in that your practice of breathing and tensing will be successful in a certain amount of time or that you will practice your visualization daily.

Here is an example of an action plan for someone who is afraid of dogs. Dogs are mostly friendly, but they have a habit of jumping up on people to get their attention. This can put a fearful person into a tizzy.

Action Plan Goal: I will no longer be afraid of dogs as long as they do not growl or snap at me.

In the goal you are saying you will not be afraid of friendly dogs. It is important that you add a caveat here. Your fight or flight reaction will save you from danger when dealing with attacking dogs as opposed to friendly dogs that way. I would include a list of actions that would render the dog unfriendly:

- Snarling dogs
- Growling dogs
- Lunging dogs

Then I would add what to do if I encountered an angry dog like this:

- Get to enclosed area or high space as quickly as possible.
- Use whatever you have to keep the dog's teeth away. Use a brief case, purse, lunch box, garbage lid, large branch, shoe to the face, etc.
- While fending off the attack I will move toward an enclosed area or towards others who can help me.

STEPS

When I see a friendly dog I will:

1. Start breathing exercises. I will breathe in through my nose using my diaphragm to the count of 8. I will hold my breath to a count of 8 and I will exhale out of my mouth to a count of 8. I will do this as long as it takes to calm myself.
2. I will start tensing exercises while I breathe. I will start by relaxing the muscles in my neck and gradually progress to my feet.
3. I will go to my calm place, which can be anything that is calming and relaxing to you. As a former pro gamer, my calm place is a magical kingdom where all evil has been eradicated, anything is possible and the forces of good prevail eternally. Be sure to come up with something that is compelling and relaxing for you.

4. I will reason with my fear and ascertain if touching the dog will cause harm.
   - Is the dog waging his tail? If he is wagging his tail, he does not feel threatened by me.
   - Does the dog look happy to see me? If he does, he must be friendly.
   - Is the dog growling? If he is, I should find something to protect myself, but if he isn't, I should stay calm.
   - Is the dog nuzzling me gently? If he is, he wants me to pet him and I will offer my hand with my palm down in a non-threatening manner for him to sniff. Then I will pet him.

5. I will take control and do what I have to make the situation better by:
   - Telling the owner I am afraid and have him remove the dog.
   - Extend my hand so the dog can sniff me.
   - Pet the dog.
   - Give the dog a treat.

6. I will celebrate by going out for an ice cream cone and pat myself on the back for not giving into fear. If I go a month consistently overcoming my fears, then I will treat myself to a professional massage.

It is as simple as that!

Take a look at this YouTube video, How To Be confident – Overcome Fear and Anxiety in Seconds by Aaron Nunez. This video sums up just about everything for those that have fear but want to be successful in life.

Conclusion

I hope this book was able to help you to overcome any fear that may pop up in your life.

The next step is to do your exercises, eat healthy, take your supplements, use visualization, try some hypnosis and make an action plan to combat fear. Overcoming fear takes some practice and patience. It doesn't happen overnight. It takes preparation and understanding. Avoid thinking about your fears when they are not present. Severely fearful people tend to fixate and become obsessed with their fear, creating an endless loop in their brain which is counterproductive. Instead of focusing on the fear, fixate on positive solutions, affirmations and goals. Banish thoughts of what scare you and occupy your mind with positive activities and thoughts.

Eventually, you may no longer have to depend on your action plan and you will automatically fight back fear. Once you overcome your fear you will begin to realize that spending your life being afraid is a waste of your precious time on this planet. Face your fears and life will be that much better!

Finally, if you discovered at least one thing that has helped you or that you think would be beneficial to someone else, be sure to take a few seconds to easily post a quick positive review. As an author, your positive feedback is desperately needed. Your highly valuable five star reviews are like a river of golden joy flowing through a sunny forest of mighty trees and beautiful flowers! *To do your good deed in making the world a better place by helping others with your valuable insight, just leave a nice review.*

My Other Books and Audio Books
www.AcesEbooks.com

Peak Performance Books

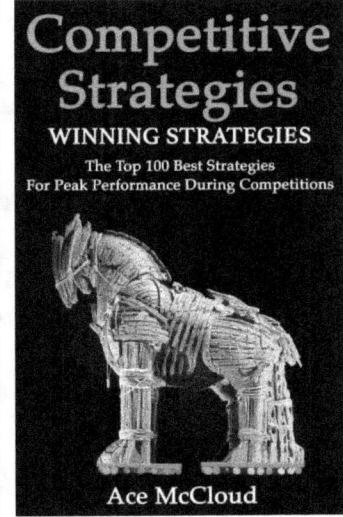

Health Books

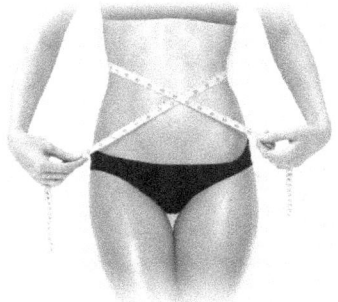 

Be sure to check out my audio books as well!

 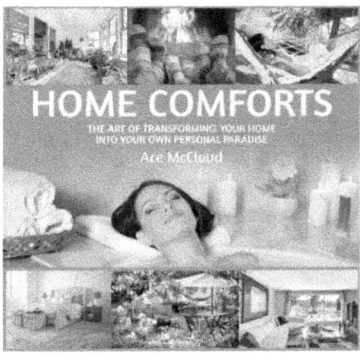 

Check out my website at: **www.AcesEbooks.com** for a complete list of all of my books and high quality audio books. I enjoy bringing you the best knowledge in the world and wish you the best in using this information to make your journey through life better and more enjoyable! **Best of luck to you!**

www.ingramcontent.com/pod-product-compliance
Lightning Source LLC
Chambersburg PA
CBHW051430070526
44584CB00023B/3665